PEACEKEEPERS

Empowering Youth Using Restorative Practices

~ AN IMPLEMENTATION MANUAL ~

JEN WILLIAMS

This publication is designed to provide accurate and authoritative information in regard to the subject matter covered. It is sold with the understanding that the publisher is not engaged in rendering psychological, physical, legal or other professional services.

If expert assistance or counseling is needed, the services of a competent professional should be sought.

The forms, scripts and cards listed on page vi can be duplicated for personal use but may not be reproduced for any other purposes without permission of the author.

Contact Jen Williams at peacekeepers.jenwilliams@gmail.com for a download link containing the forms, script and cards.

Contact Jen Williams at:
peacekeepers.jenwilliams@gmail.com

Copyright @2021 by Jen Williams

All rights reserved

ISBN 978-1-7376619-0-0

Dedication

To all the students whose lives have been touched by the Peacekeeper Program. I am truly blessed that you trusted and allowed the process to empower you.

To my friends and family. I am forever grateful for your encouragement and support.

To my editor, better known as Dad. I thank you for your excitement to join me in this endeavor and your patience while reading the many versions with a critical eye.

To Jen Moyer, my training partner. I have learned so much from you and admire our shared view of all things restorative.

To Melody Templeton and Annette Murray. I appreciate your expertise and guidance through the book writing process. You helped me find my way.

To my IIRP family. I continue to seek knowledge to improve my practice because of the worldwide restorative community that you established.

PEACEKEEPERS

"Peace cannot be kept by force. It can only be achieved by understanding."
~Albert Einstein

If you are exploring the possibility of starting a Peacekeeper Program, you're in the right place. This guide will help you bring the benefits of Restorative Practices to your setting. It has made an impact in my setting and promises to make a difference in yours.

The stages of the butterfly, denoting each section, represent the purposeful progression for the development of this program. Each section of this manual has an important role as it unfolds the process. The goal is to give students wings to become compassionate facilitators of reconciliation.

A Peacekeeper Program can run successfully at any education level. My experience is at the middle school level, and I show that perspective and experience throughout this manual. Any caring adult who works with young people may find this manual helpful. You can implement this model in schools, faith-based organizations, and any youth-centered group. Consider the impact of a program where youth are at the helm. This manual has its foundation in Restorative Practices. You may wish to attend a training through the International Institute of Restorative Practices (www.iirp.edu).

JEN WILLIAMS

Sample Forms

Peacekeeper Application 31

Peacekeeper Confidentiality Statement 47

Conflict Exploration Activity Picture Cards 85

Peacekeeper Referral 100

Peacekeeper Conference Pre-Meeting 102

Peacekeeper Facilitator/Notetaker Rubric 106

Participant Behavior Rubric 107

The Peacekeeper Conference Script 108

Peacekeeper Conference Agreement 116

Follow-Up Meeting Notes 118

End-of-Year Peacekeeper Program Evaluation 120

These forms, scripts and cards listed can be duplicated for personal use but may not be reproduced for any other purposes without permission of the author.

Contact Jen Williams at peacekeepers.jenwilliams@gmail.com for a download link containing the forms, script and cards.

Table of Contents

Getting Started 1
- Youth as Valuable Leaders 3
- Students Help Mold the Program 7

Program Development 11
- Why I Started the Peacekeeper Program 12
- Why I Stuck With It 15
- Student Stories 16
- The Hidden Potential For Students 20

Things to Consider 27
- Choosing Students for the Peacekeeper Training Program 29
- Administration Support 32
- Ongoing Training Time 33
- Peacekeeper Conference Tracker 34
- Establish Referral Sources 36
- Getting the Word Out to Staff, Students and the Community 37
- Structure the Year 38
- Timeline 39

Training 41
- Team-Building 43
- Establish Group Norms 44
- Confidentiality 46
- Strengthen the Group Community 48

1. Twizzler Tie 50
   2. Balloon Pass 52
   3. Marshmallow Challenge 54
   4. Zombie Apocalypse 56
   Divide into Peacekeeper Teams 60

Learn the Concepts 63
   Fundamental Hypothesis 66
   Social Discipline Window 68
   Compass of Shame 70
   Fishbowl Circle 72
   Fair Process 74
   Student Restorative Practices Continuum 76
   Friendly Talk 78
   Empathy vs. Sympathy 79
   Peacekeeper Affective Questions 80
   Conflict Exploration Activity 82
   Small Conversations 89
   Circles 90
   Peacekeeper Conference 91

Putting It All Together 93
   From Referral to Follow-up 96
   Peacekeeper Conference Script 104

Bibliography 123

About the Author 127

Getting Started

PEACEKEEPERS

Youth as Valuable Leaders

Society views adults as the experts in the lives of youth, but rarely does it allow youth the opportunity to show that they are capable of being experts in their own lives. Youth need to be able to express themselves to caring adults who can help advocate for their needs.

"When adults in children's lives act as referees and judges, adults place children in a dependent position and deprive them of opportunities to learn valuable self-regulation and social skills. The more students master and use the integrative negotiation and mediation procedures, the more they independently regulate their own behavior and the less monitoring and control is required by adults." (Johnson & Johnson, 2001, p. 22)

All students are valuable resources that can be used to strengthen the school community. DuPaul, McGoey & Yugar (1997, p. 635) state that "peer-mediated interventions have been found as effective as adult-mediated programming in enhancing the academic and behavioral competence of students with BD (behavior disorders)."

Ann Schumacher (2014) suggests that adolescent girls involved in circles in urban high schools across the globe develop empathy skills with classmates, which fosters a new-found confidence and self-awareness in them. The girls support each other and find commonalities when sharing their stories.

Each year, Peacekeepers include several students with tough home lives. These students report personal growth in the areas of self-confidence, responsibility, and trustworthiness after their participation in the program.

Since there is limited research in using students as facilitators for a restorative conference, I aim to share my experience with empowering students in the Peacekeeper Program. It is important to share this knowledge so that other educators take risks of allowing students the chance to lead conversation to respond to harm. As I heard Rick Phillips say at the IIRP School Climate Symposium, "Students are waiting for us to give them the opportunities to be the leaders we want them to be and they want to be." (July 2015)

"For there is always light if only we're brave enough to see it, if only we're brave enough to be it."

　　　　　　　　　　　- Amanda Gorman

Students Help Mold the Program

Youth are empowered when we give them a voice and allow them to be experts in their own lives. Rick Phillips, founder of the Safe School Ambassadors® Program in California, said, "Children are candles waiting to be lit." They thrive when people in authority unleash their empowering potential. Our goal is to teach young people the skills to ignite that potential. It is okay to give kids the keys to drive Peacekeeping.

Goodwin & Young (2013) urge adults to value young voices as relevant in the current moment. They state that young people are seen by adults as "human becomings" and not "human beings" who have "a viewpoint that is yet to be relevant" (p. 354).

Students are the foundation of the Peacekeeper Program. I approach my program with an administrative lens and embrace the perspective of students to ensure their buy-in and growth.

I ask students to give feedback regarding the program in the **End-of-Year Peacekeeper Program Evaluation** *(see page 120).* If students are not satisfied, they may become disinterested or unwilling to help, which ultimately means that other students may not get the help they need.

From this feedback, I look at ways to improve the program. I might have discussions with administration to consider potential changes as well as ways to expand the program.

Here's an example: Peacekeepers provided feedback while learning the conference script and said it was too hard to understand. This made sense, because in its original form it was intended for use with adult facilitators. As a result of student feedback, we now take time to go through the script line-by-line, editing as necessary, so that it is easier to read and understand. With the blessing of the author of the restorative script, Terry O'Connell, *(see picture on next page)* we change the script.

In order for your program to be successful, it is essential to allow students to guide the process. What *you* think is necessary, might be completely unnecessary for students.

Peacekeepers meet Terry O'Connell, the author of the restorative script.

Program Development

Why I Started the Peacekeeper Program

At about my 10th year as a middle school counselor, I began feeling a sense of burn-out, from frustration, like chasing my tail. Here's why. The issues I was attempting to address ran the gamut from supporting a student with a friend being angry with them to advocating for a student to be evaluated for potential self-harm. The crisis situations filled my time, and minor conflicts seemed to get in the way. I approached administration with an idea that would be a win-win for both myself and the school.

I offered to teach a course with the hopes of starting a group to address low-level infractions of student behavior in the building. I used restorative practices as a framework and add Social and Emotional Learning (SEL) and leadership lessons to the mix. At the time, I was starting coursework at the International Institute for Restorative Practices. My coursework and the Mediation and Conflict Resolution (MCR) course married quite nicely. I found a new focus, a spark to help me out of burnout.

Program Development

It took several years to establish a solid program, and many bumps came with that. I started collecting data and building my curriculum, resources and protocols. Each year, students committed to Peacekeeping in 8th grade and were eager to help their peers. I complemented my coursework with becoming a licensed trainer with IIRP and also trained the staff yearly to support the building's restorative mission. Students presented at the World Conference at IIRP, to the School Board, and at the reception of the honorary designation of Schools to Watch. In the first year of the program, we completed 6 conferences and sharply increased to completing over 20 each consecutive year.

In my tenure as an educator, it has been rare to find students in leadership roles at the middle level who truly are stakeholders in the programs. Students hold leadership roles in student council, musical groups, service learning, and athletics, but have not traditionally had a voice in disciplinary matters.

PEACEKEEPERS

Rick Phillips, a leader in student empowerment, said at the International Institute for Restorative Practices World Conference (October 2015), "Young people are ready and eager to have a tool to help the people they care about." In his Safe School Ambassadors® Program students are trained with skills to help social discourse in the school community. I was intrigued by this because the Peacekeeper Program is somewhat similar.

Any student can participate as a Peacekeeper if given the opportunity and support along the way. Anderson Williams (Dary and Pickeral, 2013) challenges us to change the way we relate to youth. He recommends that we empower students to be facilitators and to have a voice. He also said that we cannot assume that students are less knowledgeable than we are.

Why I Stuck With It

I have to admit, when I started the Peacekeeper Program, I never imagined the impact it would have on me. Year after year, the end of the year picnic was filled with tears, as a proud mom would have. These were tears of joy that students have shown tremendous growth from the time they start the MCR class to their last facilitation as a Peacekeeper. Since I open the program for any student to participate, the stories of growth fill my heart.

I will share four stories from students in the program who impacted my life. I've changed their names to protect their identities.

Student Stories

Annie

Annie was new to our building, she came to us as a fifth grader with angry outbursts and an IEP for emotional support. She often did not have the words to express her feelings and shut down regularly. Sometimes it was in the middle of the hallway, other times in the office that she curled up in the fetal position unable to speak. She would scream at staff and other students. Annie was really struggling.

Over time, her IEP teacher and I built relationships with Annie. She started to use words when she was upset and slowly began to advocate for herself. As course selections approached, Annie wanted to try the MCR course to be a Peacekeeper. I wanted to give her a chance. Well, Annie showed that beneath her emotional issues, she was a leader, not afraid to speak up and advocate for the good of the group. She navigated tough conversations and added stories to support students she was helping. She went on to high school where she chaired several student groups and would come back to our building to help students in the emotional support class with self-care techniques.

Program Development

Bobby

Bobby had learning needs, supported with an IEP. He presented as disheveled, unorganized, and hygiene was not a priority. He never completed his homework, but contributed to the conversation in class. He seemed to be left to care for himself. As he participated in training, Bobby shared that his parents were going through a divorce and that the skills he learned in MCR were helpful with conversations at home. He was always eager to lead facilitations or classroom announcements. The program helped him be grounded in a purpose when home was so unsteady. He said he felt part of the Peacekeeper family.

Chris

Chris presented as anxious and paralyzed by anxiety. He often wanted to contribute but did not follow through. He was juggling many activities and, as it turned out, emotions about his true identity. He went to the high school and came out to his friends and ultimately his family. He told the administration that he learned skills from the Peacekeeper Program to help find words to use when facing his truth.

Dani

Dani was shy and quiet. She never wanted to facilitate or lead discussions. She hid on the side lines, eager to help behind the scenes. She had no problems making signs, writing announcements, taking notes or greeting students at the Peace Room, but leading conversation took her way out of her comfort zone. At our end of year picnic, we always share our takeaways from the year. I have a toy microphone as a talking piece, and typically kids fight over who is first to use it. I was shocked when Dani wanted to be one of the first to share. She stood up in front of 20 people, grabbed the mic, and spoke about her love of the program. I captured a picture of her that day and have it in my office. She is laughing and holding the microphone, owning the moment.

The Hidden Potential For Students

This program includes students from every social group, learning ability, and family dynamic. In particular, there are increasing numbers of students with learning disabilities who sign up to be a Peacekeeper. At first, I was curious how students who struggle with peers would handle the responsibility as a Peacekeeper. Some even accessed the program when they found themselves in conflict as a younger student.

Maurice J. Elias (2004) finds that most students with learning disabilities have social skill deficits. They struggle to be accepted by peers, often get teased for their deficits with learning, and they lack the skills to pick up social nuances. Interacting with others is a major hurdle for some of them. The article describes findings from brain research that a connection between language deficits and social difficulties exists. It also evaluates several specific skills that educators say "students need in order to put their knowledge to productive use and live as responsible citizens" (Elias, 2004, p.54).

Program Development

The skills that are incorporated in the Peacekeeper curriculum from those findings include:

- *Recognizing Emotion in Self and Others*

- *Regulating and Managing Strong Emotions*

- *Recognizing Strengths and Areas Of Need*

Recognizing Emotion in Self and Others

This is essential to help students increase feelings vocabulary to include words other than sad, glad or mad. Elias says that feeling mad leads to externalizing and acting out, while feeling sad leads to resignation and learned helplessness. Working through Peacekeeper Affective Questions (PAQs—*see page 81*), writing reflections to picture cards *(see page 85-88)* and classroom role playing help develop an awareness of emotions in themselves and others.

A student during Peacekeeper training initially presented as withdrawn and had previous suicidal thoughts. He blossomed into an outgoing and confident student, often sharing valuable insight during formal conferences in the Peace Room*. All students in the class express their affective responses to videos, role plays, and team building activities and are seen as equals in the social dynamics of the training.

---

*The term *Peace Room* is used throughout this manual when referring to the space in which the Peacekeepers work. In my setting, it is a dedicated space that is decorated with calming lights and hand-shaped chairs. You may wish to find a space similar for your work.

Regulating and Managing Strong Emotions

When students act out, there is a reason. They get frustrated easily, and they don't always express their feelings in appropriate or safe ways. During the Peacekeeper training, students create posters about conflict showing what it is, how it escalates, and what emotions contribute to it. Project groups are carefully selected based on social needs so that each participant has an opportunity to contribute to the group. Students watch pop culture movie clips to observe how conflicts escalate, and students create their own role plays to illustrate escalation and also ways to de-escalate conflicts when they occur.

Recognizing Strengths and Areas of Need

Students find success when focusing on their strengths. Students bring their own gifts to the Peacekeeper Program. Once trained as Peacekeepers, students are given a choice of which role they will take during interventions (greeter, notetaker, and facilitator). This ensures all students have a place in the program. No student is excluded unless by his or her choice.

Program Development

Things to Consider

PEACEKEEPERS

Choosing Students for the Peacekeeper Training Program

1. Allow all students to apply, including those with learning and behavior needs. I include everyone because students in the program gain valuable life skills as I mentioned before. There is a place for everyone.

2. Don't just include "good" kids, those already in school leadership roles, in the program. There needs to be a representation of the student body, including influential leaders and those who have a voice with groups that may not make the best decisions all the time.

3. Have students sign up through the course selection process. That way, their parents are part of the process.

4. Meet with each student to give them an application. Assess who may need some encouragement along the way.

5. Celebrate the students moving forward for Peacekeeper Training by sending a congratulatory letter of acceptance into the program.

6. Train as many students as possible. Give students the opportunity to fully participate. Some students may not want to be a Peacekeeper at the end of the training and that is ok. It is a time commitment away from their lunch and classes.

PEACEKEEPERS

Page to the right shows an example of an application, one that I developed for my program.

Peacekeeper Application

Things to Consider

Student Name: _____   Team: _____

The Peacekeeper Program is a program at [insert school name] that helps students resolve conflicts using a Restorative Conference. Peacekeepers must have a good work ethic, a willingness to help, be willing to lead, have integrity (be able to keep confidentiality) and also have strong engagement in school. Peacekeepers must be trained on [insert date of training] in order to participate next school year. During 8th grade, Peacekeepers attend weekly meetings during flex and are assigned to teams. Each team works about 1 time every other week during related arts. Please answer the following questions on a separate piece of paper to be considered for a Peacekeeper position next year. There is a maximum of [insert number of students you can accept] accepted. All applications must be given to [insert adult advisor's name] in the office, with a parent signature, by [insert date due].

Question 1:
Why are you applying to be a Peacekeeper? Include skills and strengths you have to offer and how you will support the program.

Question 2:
How would your friends describe you as a person? What is your role in your friend group? (leader, mediator, comedian, cheerleader)?

Question 3:
In your own words, what is integrity? Why would this quality be important as a Peacekeeper?

Question 4:
Describe a time you supported a friend/family member through a conflict. What was your strategy? What went well? What could have been done differently? Was the conflict resolved?

Please review this process with your parent/guardian. If they approve your involvement in this program and to the commitment for next school year, they need to sign here.

_____   _____
Parent's Printed Name   Parent's Signature

Contact Jen Williams, author of *Peacekeepers, An Implementation Manual for Empowering Youth Using Restorative Practices,* at peacekeepers.jenwilliams@gmail.com for a download link to this Peacekeeper Application.

Administration Support

It is imperative that the building administration supports the program and works with you to integrate it into the school community. The program needs to be part of the behavior support/discipline system so that there is a sense of importance and value in it. There needs to be designated time and space for the group to work. This might be during a common advisory/homeroom time. In my case, I met with the Peacekeepers during their homeroom time once a week as a large group. They did their prep work with the students during their lunches and facilitated conferences during their related arts times. Nothing lined up perfectly, but it was an expectation put forth by the building administration that an invitation to the Peace Room was serious, and students are expected to attend unless a test or an assessment was being given at that time.

"In time of crisis, the wise build bridges, while the foolish build barriers. We must find a way to look after one another as if we were one single tribe."
—T'Challa, Black Panther

Ongoing Training Time

In order for a program to thrive, there needs to be high support, which means, I am physically present in everything they do. I commit to meeting with the Peacekeepers weekly. We meet in a circle. Part of the time is spent going over the cases for the week, and the other part is spent either team-building or reviewing skills. I always start with a quick go-around. Then, I ask Peacekeeper groups to reflect back on a facilitation: what worked and where is support needed.

It is important for their peers in other groups to offer support. I also debrief with groups after each facilitation to provide direct feedback in the moment. The questions, "What is something to celebrate?" and "What is an area of growth?" are often asked.

As a counselor, weeks can go by without a "positive" in my job. I typically am responding to crisis or other student needs. I look forward to time in the Peace Room each week. I didn't realize how much the program fills my bucket until it was missing.*

---

*During the 2020-2021 school year, the Peacekeeper Program was unable to run due to COVID restrictions.

Peacekeeper Conference Tracker

Data collection is an essential piece to the program. Data helps administrators see the effects of the program. It also provides central office administration data for our state report of building safety. I keep track of the amount of cases completed each year, how many students were involved and the agreements that are developed. Since starting the program, the number of suspensions has dropped in my building.

Peacekeeper Conference Tracker				
Case Number	Group Names	Date	Meeting Type	
1	Majestic Monkeys	10/17/19	Peacekeeper Conference	
2	Peaceful Penguins	10/22/19	Pre-Meeting	
3	Friendship Flamingos	10/22/19	Peacekeeper Conference	
4	Peaceful Ducks	10/29/19	Pre-Meeting	
5	Majestic Monkeys	11/1/19	Pre-Meeting	
6	Peaceful Penguins	11/1/19	Pre-Meeting	
7	Friendship Flamingos	1/16/20	Pre-Meeting	
8	Peaceful Ducks	12/10/19	Pre-Meeting	
9	Friendship Flamingos	1/28/2020	Pre-Meeting	
10	Majestic Monkeys	1/28/2020	Pre-Meeting	

Things to Consider

Below is a spreadsheet I kept during the 2019-20 school year. In addition to what I described on the previous page, it shows the sequence of each case. I have files for each case numbered in a portable file box. I recommend a similar system to maintain confidentiality if your Peace Room space is not the same as your office/classroom space. I took the box with me whenever I met with Peacekeepers and keep it locked in my office during other times.

Date	Meeting Type	Date	Meeting Type
1/10/20	Participant Follow-Up	1/22/20	Additional Peace Room Time
10/23/19	Peacekeeper Conference	1/13/20	Participant Follow-Up
10/24/19	Peacekeeper Conference	1/16/20	Participant Follow-Up
10/31/19	Peacekeeper Conference	1/14/20	Participant Follow-Up
11/7/19	Peacekeeper Conference	1/16/20	Participant Follow-Up
11/6/19	Peacekeeper Conference	1/13/20	Participant Follow-Up
Parent Declined			
12/13/19	Peacekeeper Conference	1/14/2020	Participant Follow-Up
1/31/2020	Peacekeeper Conference		
1/29/2020	Peacekeeper Conference		

Establish Referral Sources

Referrals come from various sources. The building principals, counselors, and behavior coordinators for each grade primarily make referrals. Sometimes students self-refer, and parents might ask their child to participate in the Peacekeeper Conference.

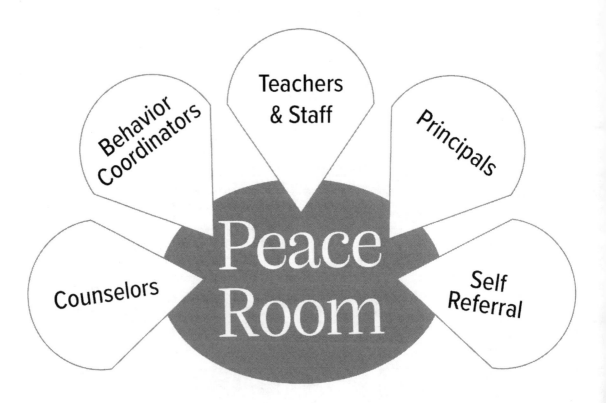

Things to Consider

Getting the Word Out to Staff, Students and the Community

The Peacekeepers are always eager to let others know about their program. They make announcements and host tours for students. They invite staff into conferences to experience the power of the restorative process and they host open houses for parents on conference nights. I ask parents to sign field trip permission slips and the Peacekeeper application. I also ask for their partnership in celebration and for Peace Room decor donations. Students also present at IIRP's World Conference and our school board meetings to share their experiences with the program. It is important to have a public presence to foster community support.

Structure the Year

The timeline has evolved over the years. At first, the program started with a full spring semester training course for seventh graders called Mediation and Conflict Resolution (MCR). It met every other day for 45 minutes. I started offering a 1-day training in May for 7th graders a few years ago to replace the MCR course and now I train them in September, which is ideal for everyone's time and other responsibilities.

The training teaches the main concepts of restorative practices and ends with a competency assessment of the Peacekeeper Conference script. More on that in the next section. In the fall of the 8th grade year, morning meetings begin during homeroom to focus on team-building, dividing the students into working groups, and reviewing concepts from the training.

A select group from the Peacekeepers presents at the IIRP World Conference each time it is held in Bethlehem, PA, typically in October. Those not presenting, focus on planning an open house for students and also for parents to kick off our work for the year.

A team-building trip is planned around January. The escape room trip was a top favorite for all. Then, there is an end-of-year picnic to celebrate each other and share memories from the program. Students also complete a program feedback survey as another piece of data with recommendations for program improvement.

Timeline

September: Team-building activities and training to kick off the year. Set up Peace Room

October: IIRP World Conference presentation and Peace Room Open House for students

January: Mid-Year Team-building Trip

March: Parent/Teacher Conference Night

April: Present to School Board and work on other public relations projects

June: End-of-Year Celebration Trip; complete Peacekeeper program evaluations

Training

"Happiness can be found even in the darkest of time, if one only remembers to turn on the light."

—Albus Dumbledore

Team-Building

After students sign up for a full school day training (with parent permission), I reserve the space for the day and alert the teachers of their absence. Then we spend the day getting to know one another and diving into the restorative skills that are essential for the program. Over the next several pages, I will break down the training day to give you an idea how I structure the training.

Establish Group Norms

Establishing group norms is an essential part of the training. If you skip this, unexpected challenges may arise throughout the year. It also sets the ground work for any group conflicts that might arise during the year among the Peacekeepers.

This is not about what you want as a trainer. The students must have a say in creating the norms of the process. If there is a non-negotiable (something you think is necessary to have on the list) that they don't suggest, make sure you offer it.

Some typical norms include, but are not limited to:

    a. The person with the talking piece* has the floor.

    b. What is said in here, stays in here. (confidentiality)

    c. Establish appropriate break times.

    d. Cell phones are left in your locker.

    e. Take risks, be vulnerable, be ready to grow.

    f. Have fun!

*A common object that students hold when its their turn to speak.

Training

As student suggestions are noted, each bullet point is explored for concrete explanations of what they mean to the group. For example, there was a lengthy conversation over the use of electronic devices during one training. All options and opinions were presented by the group and discussed. It was decided that students would put their devices on the back counter while in the Peace Room and only use them with my permission.

Midway through the year, several class members raised the concern that cell phones were being used during the class. I convened a circle and gave the students space to discuss the concern. The Peacekeepers reminded each other of the agreement made by the group. Students shared opinions about the topic in question. The policy was updated to include a step that they are permitted to discuss their specific needs for having a cell phone in class (e.g. family emergency) with the instructor.

Establishing group expectations at the beginning of the course helps to foster open dialogue with the classroom community and to address issues calmly and respectfully with the group. It is practicing among themselves what they expect in their Peacekeeper conferences with students.

Confidentiality

Confidentiality is discussed often in training and throughout the year. There are times when Peacekeepers are neighbors of students in the Peace Room or friends with a sibling of a student in the Peace Room. We discuss these scenarios in training and often establish a guideline that the Peacekeeper excuses him/herself from a conference with someone they know.

There have also been times when students in the Peace Room disclose that they are not safe or are participating in destructive behaviors, times when parents are contacted. The Peacekeepers understand that I may need to step in to help students be safe.

In order for any Peacekeeper to work in the Peace Room, they must sign a confidentiality agreement, like the one here.

Peacekeeper Confidentiality Statement

I promise to maintain confidentiality as a facilitator with Peacekeepers at _____.
                                  [insert school name]

I will be working with students who have conflicts, and I want to make sure their conflict is kept between those involved, myself, and _____.
                                  [insert program coordinator's name]

I want to ensure a safe place for students to talk about their conflict with the hope that they will want my help again in the future.

_____
                    [print name]

Signature: _____

Date: _____

Witness: _____

Date: _____

Contact Jen Williams, author of *Peacekeepers, An Implementation Manual for Empowering Youth Using Restorative Practices,* at peacekeepers.jenwilliams@gmail.com for a download link to the Peacekeeper Confidentiality Statement.

Strengthen the Group Community

We have all participated in community-building events. Sports teams do wall sits while singing songs to get through the pain. Church youth groups untangle a human knot. Classrooms play silent ball. All these are examples of how leaders use activities to provide opportunities for students to work together in unique ways.

I will walk you through four activities that build community with Peacekeepers. It is intentional that the activities start in pairs and grow in group size. This allows the adult facilitator to carefully observe how the group changes with each activity. You may wish to allow students to partner with a familiar person at first to find out who already have strong relationships. Then separating them for the other activities. Keep a watchful eye and take notes of what you observe.

It is important discuss the process of debriefing. This is the most important part of community building.

Do not skip this!

Debrief

After each activity, groups discuss how the activities are tied directly to their work as Peacekeepers and in their own lives. In particular, the group discusses ways these activities align with their future roles as student facilitators. The group identifies that in order to be a student facilitator the students must work together and communicate effectively.

Some questions asked of students include:

What did you specifically do or say that contributed to success?

What did you specifically do or say that hindered success?
(It is ok that things don't go as planned. Make sure students express frustrations.)

What specific learnings can you apply to the Peacekeeping process?

Over the next several pages, I provide four lesson plans with debrief questions for specific activities I use with the Peacekeepers for building unity among them.

1. Twizzler Tie

Objective: To be the first student pair to work together to tie a Twizzler candy in a knot with one hand behind their backs.

Materials: One twizzler for each student (and more for sharing after!)

Procedure:

Students pair up and be given one Twizzler piece.

On 'Go' signal, pairs attempt to tie a knot in the candy while each keeping one hand behind their back.

The goal is to be the fastest pair to tie the knot.

As the facilitator, take note of how the pairs communicate, the frustration level, and the steps they took to solve the problem.

Debrief

What did you specifically do or say that contributed to your success?
(Examples: I told my partner a specific move to make. I was able to maneuver to tie the knot.)

What did you specifically do or say that hindered your success?
(Examples: I said that this was impossible. I kept dropping the candy.)

How can you compare what you did in order to solve this problem with what we do in the Peace Room?

What skills did you use during this activity that you can apply to the Peacekeeping process?

2. Balloon Pass

Objective: To be the first group to successfully transfer the balloon around the circle using a pencil.

Materials: An unsharpened pencil for each student, one inflated balloon per group.

Procedure:

Students form two groups of at least 4-5, each student has a pencil.

Place balloon between the pencils of two students.

On 'Go' signal, students must transfer the balloon to each student, subsequently, around the circle.

The group is finished when the balloon gets back between the pencils of the students who started with it.

Rules: Balloon must be transferred to every student in the group, balloon may not touch any body parts, only one hand is allowed on the pencil, balloon may not touch the ground. If any rule is broken, balloon goes back to start.

As the facilitator, take note of how the pairs communicate, the frustration level, and the steps they took to solve the problem.

Variation: If you have a smaller group, consider working as one group, and time the group's attempt. The group can start by attempting to complete the activity, then they can try to complete the activity at a faster time.

Debrief

What did you specifically do or say that contributed to your success? *(Examples: I told my partner to hold their pencil a certain way. I was able to pass the balloon without making a mistake.)*

What did you specifically do or say that hindered your success? *(Examples: I said that I'll never be able to do this. I kept dropping the balloon.)*

How can you compare what you did in order to solve this problem with what we do in the Peace Room?

What skills that you used during this activity will you apply to the Peacekeeping process?

3. Marshmallow Challenge

Objective: Build the tallest free-standing structure in 3 minutes.

Materials: 25 marshmallows and 25 toothpicks for each small group, a measuring device, a timer

Procedure:

Divide the group into groups of 5-6 students.

Each group has 25 mini marshmallows and 25 toothpicks (partially stale marshmallows work best, just let a bag open overnight - but you may want a fresh bag for sharing a treat after the activity).

Students are given 3 minutes to plan without touching materials.

On 'Go' signal, pairs attempt to build the tallest free-standing structure in 3 minutes.

As the facilitator, take note of how the pairs communicate, the frustration level, and the steps they took to solve the problem.

Debrief

What did you specifically do or say that contributed to your success? *(Examples: I had the idea of putting two marshmallows on one toothpick. I told my group that we were doing great.)*

What did you specifically do or say that hindered your success? *(Examples: I said that this was impossible. I broke a toothpick.)*

How can you compare what you did in order to solve this problem with what we do in the Peace Room?

What skills that you used during this activity will you apply to the Peacekeeping process?

4. Zombie Apocalypse

Objective: To rank random survival items from most important to least important in order to survive. To experience debate with classmates.

Materials: Survival item cards for each group. A large board/chart paper to record the group's choices.

Procedure:

Distribute survival item cards to individual students and ask the group to identify a student to be the group's recorder.

On 'Go' signal, students debate items to be ranked.

Debate is encouraged, and all must agree on the ranking. Students may ask clarifying questions. Resist helping and limit sharing details about the scenario. This allows for more discussion among the group members.

As the facilitator, take note of how the groups communicate, the frustration level, and the steps they took to solve the problem.

Variation: You can do this as one large group and use any survival items you choose.

10 Survival Items: These are examples of the survival item cards I use with the group. They are simple drawings that I laminated. The items include compass, battery, sunscreen, metal pot, canned food, medical supplies, knife, matches, parachute and socks. Use your imagination and modify the list to meet your group's needs. *(continued on next page)*

PEACEKEEPERS

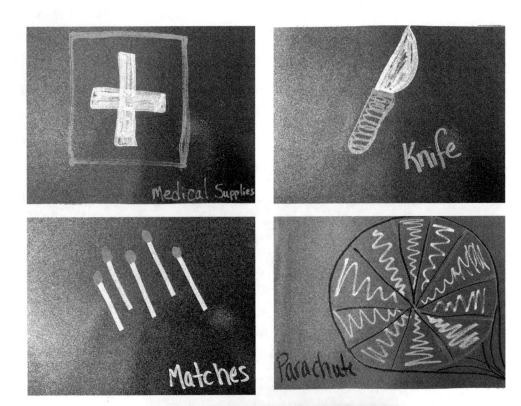

Debrief

What did you specifically do or say that contributed to your success? (*Examples: I made a statement that everyone agreed on. I was able to convince someone to change their mind.*)

What did you specifically do or say that hindered your success? (*Examples: I said that this was impossible. I would not agree to a certain ranking.*)

How can you compare what you did in order to solve this problem with what we do in the Peace Room?

What skills that you used during this activity will you apply to the Peacekeeping process?

Divide into Peacekeeper Teams

You may notice that natural leaders emerge during the team building activities. There might also be strong alliances that exist.

Divide the Peacekeepers into working groups with a balance of personalities and leadership styles. I found that four teams of four to five Peacekeepers is the most efficient and ideal for the program. This way, each team is always working on a case and each Peacekeeper can have an active role in the Peace Room.

Allow teams to develop their own names. This is how they differentiate case assignments from other teams.

The roles the Peacekeepers play are:

a. Facilitator #1 - leads the students through the script

b Facilitator #2 - supports/co-facilitates with Facilitator #1*

c. Notetaker - completes form and has students sign agreement

d. Greeter - welcomes students and give students name tags

*Please consider the following when you see the term *Facilitator* used throughout the manual. During the school year it is inevitable that Peacekeepers will be absent or held in class for some reason. The Facilitator #2 role is used only when the full team is available. Often, Facilitator #1 and the Notetaker are the primary roles. Also, the Greeter is the support person for the Notetaker.

Learn the Concepts

PEACEKEEPERS

Learn the Concepts

After some team-building and a quick break, students start learning the restorative framework that is the foundation of the Peacekeeper Program.

This section describes each restorative concept I teach in training. This manual is not meant to provide in-depth analysis of each concept. For that, I refer you to the International Institute for Restorative Practices (www.iirp.edu), which was foundational for me.

Fundamental Hypothesis

The fundamental hypothesis of restorative practices is that human beings are happier, more cooperative and productive, and more likely to make positive changes in their behavior when those in positions of authority do things with them, rather than to them or for them. *[credited to IIRP]*

# Learn the Concepts

Social Discipline Window

The goal of a restorative practitioner is to work "with" others. It is valuable for students to learn the power of working with others. It is with the knowledge of the Social Discipline Window that students can start learning the value of a restorative conference. Peacekeepers work with students to guide them towards a plan to move beyond their conflicts.

People respond best when given high support and high control. I often use the example of parenting a child who is learning to tie his/her shoes. A child gets a punishment or gets yelled at if the parent operates with a "TO" style. A parent whose style is in the "FOR" quadrant ties the shoe for the child. A "NOT" parenting style is hands off and allows the child to walk around with the shoe untied. Ideally, a parent with a restorative parenting style sits with the child and reviews the steps while the child practices tying his/her shoe. Imagine you are the child. Which style would help you learn to tie your shoes with less tears or frustration?

Learn the Concepts

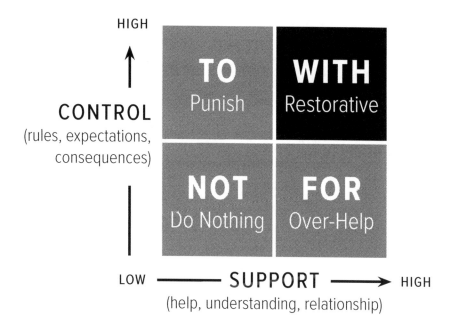

Adapted from: Wachtel, T., O'Connell, T., & Wachtel, B. (2010). Restorative justice conferencing: Real justice & the Conferencing handbook (pp. 228-230). International Institute for Restorative Practices.

Compass of Shame

Shame is an interruption of a positive affect. The Compass of Shame shows four negative ways people respond to shame. The students explore each response from examples I show in movie clips. I also ask the students how they would respond if the WiFi stopped while playing their favorite video game or watching something online. The students break into four groups and are assigned a compass point.

> *Attack other (lash out at someone)*
>
> *Attack self (self-harm)*
>
> *Avoidance (drug and alcohol use)*
>
> *Withdrawal (run away)*

Through role play, the students experience damaging responses to shame firsthand. This is important for students who mostly do the right thing and have control of their emotions. Students love playing and being silly while guessing each group's shame response.

The Peacekeeper Conference process allows students to work through shame and the behaviors that surface by holding space to tell their stories to receive understanding and empathy.

Learn the Concepts

Nathanson, 1992

Wachtel, T., O'Connell, T., & Wachtel, B. (2010). Restorative justice conferencing: Real justice & the Conferencing handbook (pp. 174-175). International Institute for Restorative Practices.

PEACEKEEPERS

Fishbowl Circle

Why is this a crowd favorite? Students lead the discussion and help each other problem solve real issues in their lives.

The general idea of a Fishbowl Circle is that the group helps brainstorm solutions for a group member in need of help.

There is a main circle that surrounds the student with the problem to be solved. To facilitate the flow of the activity there are two chairs placed next to the student in the center. As one student offers a solution, another student can sit in the second chair and wait their turn to offer a solution.

The student describes their dilemma to the group (give them two minutes max to speak) and then is quiet and remains that way throughout the process.

Select a student to be a Notetaker for the group.

Those in the outer circle with possible solutions to the dilemma take turns sitting in one of the empty chairs and sharing ideas. Then they return to their seats in the outer circle and may come back to the center, if they have additional ideas to offer. Allow five minutes for students to brainstorm possible solutions.

Learn the Concepts

The student with the dilemma may respond with a "thank you" when ideas are shared. There is no debate on what idea is good or bad, feasible or not. The group simply presents ideas for the student to consider.

If the student chooses to ask the group for an action plan, then the group helps them out. If not, the group moves on to the next student who wants help from the group.

It's fun and completely student-focused. This activity can also be used to brainstorm other things such as field trips and fundraising.

Fair Process

"Individuals are most likely to trust and cooperate freely with systems - whether they themselves win or lose by those systems - when fair process is observed." (Kim and Mauborgne, 2003).

a. Engagement (all voices are heard in decision-making)

b. Explanation (participants know the reasoning behind the decision)

c. Expectation Clarity (participants understand the decision and what is expected of them in the future)

"You must unlearn what you have learned. You will know good from bad when you are calm, at peace, passive."
—Grand Master Yoda

Learn the Concepts

As the program coordinator, it is crucial that students are actively engaged in the development and daily operations of the program. I fully explain what decisions are made, include their voices in the process, and tell them the reasons when they are not involved.

For instance, I asked students where they wanted to go for a mid-year team building/celebration trip. They suggested ideas that were individual and group activities. They wanted to play laser tag or do an escape room.

I gave students an opportunity to discuss their reasoning on both ideas and explained that the escape room was chosen for its cooperative purpose. Those that did not vote for the escape room understood the reasoning behind the choice.

Student Restorative Practices Continuum

The Student Continuum shows a progression of restorative processes that exist. From left to right, each one increases the amount of prep work and people involved. This helps us see all the ways we use restorative practices with others. It can be a simple connection with someone or a formal meeting with many pre-meetings and a script. For students, it's about developing and fixing relationships. I will explain each in more detail next.

Relationship Building

Friendly Talk	Peacekeeper Affective Questions (PAQs)
check in with others	include others to resolve concern

Learn the Concepts

Relationship Fixing

Small Conversations	Circle or Large Group	Peacekeeper Conference
discuss many topics	foster community and respond as a whole group	repair harm using a script

Adapted from: Wachtel, T., O'Connell, T., & Wachtel, B. (2010). Restorative justice conferencing: Real justice & the Conferencing handbook (Pg. 155). International Institute for Restorative Practices.

Friendly Talk

This activity develops active listening skills. I first model what active listening looks like (open posture, appropriate eye contact, nodding to show interest). Then students practice the skills. They face each other like in the picture below. The group completes four to five rounds, sixty seconds each round. They introduce themselves to their partner and discuss new topics each time. Begin with safe and easy topics. The outer circle rotates to the right after each round. Active listening is a skill that needs development because students communicate virtually as a preferred mode. Be prepared for awkward moments and giggles. This is definitely something out of their comfort zones.

Possible topics include:

a. favorite pizza topping

b. people that live in your house

c. favorite time of year

d. best trip ever taken

e. favorite peaceful place

Empathy vs. Sympathy

It is important that students understand the difference between empathy and sympathy when working with others.

With empathy, we seek to understand and imagine ourselves living the other person's experience, with phrases like, "It sounds like that was really hard for you. Tell me more about that."

With sympathy, we often have pity for the person and risk belittling them or causing a shame response with responses like, "I know how you feel." or "You must be feeling _____." or "What a shame."

"Empathy fuels connection.
Sympathy drives disconnection."
~ Dr. Brené Brown

Peacekeeper Affective Questions

It is imperative that students use language that is supportive and productive. The Peacekeeper Affective Questions (PAQs) give them tools and a starting point for conversations with others. Notice that the question, "why?" is not there. When we ask, "why", it can cause resentment and a shame response because the person is asked to justify a decision or stance they made.

As a practice activity, have students break into triads. Give the group possible conflicts to explore or allow them to come up with their own. Students take turns asking the PAQs to the other students. Make sure all students understand each question. They often struggle with "who has been affected?" and may need extra examples of this.

Students often contribute in some way to both sides of a conflict and find value in working through all of the PAQs.

I suggest having the PAQs posted around the Peace Room for the year to be quick references for the students.

Learn the Concepts

The PAQs for both the offender and the person harmed are listed here:

1. What happened?

2. What were you thinking about at the time?

3. What have you thought about since?

4. Who has been affected by what you have done? In what way?

5. What did you think when you realized what had happened?

6. What impact has this incident had on you and others?

7. What has been the hardest thing for you?

8. What do you need to do to make things right? What do you need to feel safe from this incident?

Next, I will describe an activity to explore conflict using the Peacekeeper Affective Questions (PAQs).

PEACEKEEPERS

Conflict Exploration Activity

Objective: Peacekeepers review and practice the Peacekeeper Affective Questions (PAQs) and brainstorm possible solutions to varied and common conflict scenarios.

Materials: Notebook paper, poster paper, tape, Conflict Exploration Activity Picture Cards, markers

Procedure:

Peacekeepers pair up to write stories using the PAQs* *(see page 81)* while referring to Conflict Exploration Activity Picture Cards *(use samples found on page 85-88 or create your own)*.

Pairs attach stories to chart paper and hang them around the Peace Room.

Peacekeepers do a gallery walk while referring to PAQs again. They individually make suggestions for possible solutions on the chart paper for repairing the harm described in the stories.

Coming back together as a group, Peacekeepers review the possible solutions and find themes to create possible "solution posters" for the Peace Room. These posters help participants in future Peacekeeper Conferences think of solutions if they get stuck.

---

*Leave out question number eight: "What do you need to do to make things right? What do you need to feel safe from this incident?".

Learn the Concepts

Some possible solutions might be:

a. apologize

b. avoid each other on social media

c. replace the broken item

d. use words, not fists, when you get angry

e. involve an adult to help

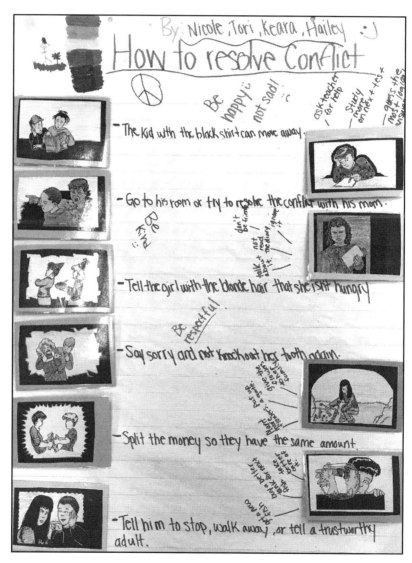

A sample of a solutions poster created during a Conflict Exploration Activity.

Debrief

What came easily to you as you worked through this activity?
(Examples: It was easy for me to think up a story. It was easy to think up solutions with a partner.)

What was difficult for you as you worked through this activity?
(Examples: I couldn't remember all the PAQs. I could only come up with one solution.)

What did you learn about yourself today?
(Answers will vary.)

Note: I find it helpful to keep the conflict stories to use when practicing the Peacekeeper Conference script.

Contact Jen Williams, author of *Peacekeepers, An Implementation Manual for Empowering Youth Using Restorative Practices,* at peacekeepers.jenwilliams@gmail.com for a download link containing the Conflict Activity Picture Cards.

Conflict Exploration Activity Picture Cards

PEACEKEEPERS

Learn the Concepts

PEACEKEEPERS

Small Conversations

Typically, adults use this practice more often to gain a quick understanding from a student who is in a conflict with another student. It could also be a quick way to check in with students about homework completion, making a plan for extra help, preparing a student for a fire alarm, etc.

In the Peace Room, we use small conversations to prepare for a conference, to meet with participants individually. The Peacekeepers find out if the students in conflict want to participate and what they want from their time in the Peace Room. This process is explained on page 103.

"You and I are a team. There is nothing more important than our friendship."
~Mike Wazowski, Monsters Inc.

PEACEKEEPERS

Circles

The Peacekeepers meet regularly in a circle. We train, have weekly check-ins, and run conferences in a circle. The circle allows everyone to have a voice. No one can hide, but they also feel connected and safe to share ideas with the group.

Peacekeeper Conference

The restorative process of the Peacekeeper Conference brings people together who are in conflict and helps them come up with their own solution for ending the conflict, and restoring any harm done.

Students at the middle level often have conflicts and they are developmentally focused only on themselves. The Peacekeeper Conference allows everyone involved in a conflict a chance to explore who was involved and how they were involved. It helps students explore solutions and develop a plan to make things right for those involved in the conflict.

A Peacekeeper Conference requires preparation, following a script, and developing a plan to repair harm with participants. Students who run Peacekeeper Conferences need to have specific training to facilitate purposeful conversation with their peers.

I share specifics for teaching the script on pages 104-113 in the "Putting it all Together" section.

Putting It All Together

PEACEKEEPERS

Putting It All Together

This next section provides a step-by-step explanation of the Peacekeeper Program from a referral to the Peackeeper Conference.

From Referral to Follow-up

1. Referral received by Program Coordinator.

2. Program Coordinator assigns the case to the next available Peacekeeper Team and adds the case to the **Peacekeeper Conference Tracker** *(see pages 34-35).*

3. Program Coordinator meets with the assigned team to ensure confidentiality and to explain the conflict to the Peacekeepers. Allow five to 10 minutes.

4. The Pre-Meeting. Allow ten minutes for each student interviewed.

    a. The Program Coordinator schedules the Pre-Meeting during the Peacekeepers' lunch time. These meetings are held in the office conference room since it is next to my office. You may want to have everything in the Peace Room.

    b. The Peacekeeper Team, along with students in conflict, complete the **Peacekeeper Conference Pre-Meeting** form *(see page 102).*

    c. If students all agree to participate in the Peacekeeper Conference the Program Coordinator schedules time in the Peace Room.

    d. If any student involved in the conflict does not wish to participate the Program Coordinator makes note of that and refers the students to their respective counselors/administrator. The Peacekeepers get the next available case.

5. Program Coordinator arranges passes for all students involved in the upcoming Peacekeeper Conference and makes staff aware.

Note: I sit outside of the circle so that the students can speak freely with the Peacekeepers. I keep a close ear to the conversation and interject only if I feel the conversation is not being productive.

Putting It All Together

6. The Peacekeeper Conference (see pages 108-113)
Allow 30-45 minutes.

   a. The Peacekeeper Team makes sure the Peace Room is ready:

      1. Turn on lighting.

      2. Set out name tags (use student first names only).

      3. Arrange the exact amount of chairs needed into a circle.

   b. The Greeter welcomes students to the Peace Room and provides them with name tags.

   c. The Facilitators seat everyone in specific spots around the circle with the configuration below as a guide.

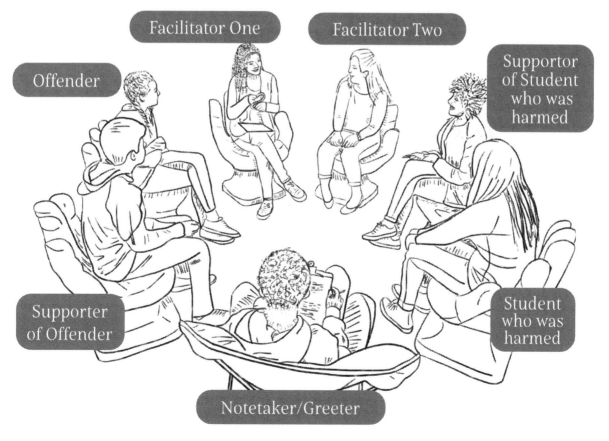

d. The Facilitators guide the students through the script, asking questions along the way to deepen their understanding of the conflict. They do not offer advice and only suggest solutions if the group is stuck.

e. The Notetaker takes notes about the conflict and writes the **Peacekeeper Conference Agreement** *(see page 116).*

f. The students sign the agreement and put their name tags on the peace sign as a way of "breaking bread", a celebration of their work together. Typically, there would be a reception for all participants to gather after a formal conference. We decided to use a symbolic metal peace sign to put name tags on.

7. The Peacekeepers stay for a quick 5-minute check-in on how the conference went, offering each other feedback. Students need this support. They need to be able to talk it out.

8. The Program Coordinator sets up a Participant Follow-Up Meeting for two weeks after the Peacekeeper Conference.

Putting It All Together

9. The Participant Follow-Up Meeting

    a. The Peacekeeper Team meets with the students and completes the **Follow-Up Meeting Notes** (*see page 118*).

    b. Another conference is set up in the Peace Room at the request of either of the students involved in the conflict.

The next several pages provides the tools and explainations for each step of the process. You may reproduce any page for your use with students.

PEACEKEEPERS

Peacekeeper Referral

Your Name:_____ Grade: _____ Date of Incident: _____

Who is involved:

Person(s) causing harm: _____

Person(s) being harmed: _____

How often is this happening?

☐ It is the first time   ☐ Daily   ☐ Weekly   ☐ Monthly

Where did it happen?

[ ] school   [ ] online   [ ] during after school activity   [ ] on the bus   [ ] at home   [ ] youth center/church

What Happened?

☐ Someone is teasing me and/or my friend

☐ Someone hurt me and/or my friend

☐ Someone took something from me and/or a friend

☐ I am in conflict with someone

☐ Someone threatened to hurt me and/or my friend

☐ Something happened online that is causing issues in school

What steps have you already taken to resolve the issue?

☐ I told them to stop

☐ I told an adult at school (teacher/counselor/bus driver/nurse)

☐ I told my parent

☐ I ignored them/walked away

☐ I met with my teacher with the other student(s) to resolve it

Would you be willing to go to the Peace Room to work it out with the student?

☐ Yes

☐ No

Please provide us with more information about your concern on the back of this paper.

Contact Jen Williams, author of *Peacekeepers, An Implementation Manual for Empowering Youth Using Restorative Practices,* at peacekeepers.jenwilliams@gmail.com for a download link containing the Peacekeeper Referral.

Putting It All Together

The **Peacekeeper Referral** form at left is the starting point in the Peacekeeper Conference. It gives the person harmed the first step in telling his/her story about what happened. The office gives me referrals to determine if they are appropriate for the Peace Room. If I feel they meet the criteria for the Peacekeeper Conference, I set up a Pre-Meeting.

The Peacekeeper Conference is a place to support low level incidences such as name calling, exclusion, teasing, etc. I strongly suggest talking with your administration on what behaviors meet your specific criteria that the Peacekeepers support. Avoid violent, sexual and drug related offenses.

PEACEKEEPERS

Peacekeeper Conference Pre-Meeting

Case # _____   Date: _____

Peacekeeper team assigned _____

Students involved in conflict	Role in Conflict	Agreed to participate?
_____	_____	_____
_____	_____	_____
_____	_____	_____
_____	_____	_____
_____	_____	_____
_____	_____	_____
_____	_____	_____

___ Ask participants to tell you what happened (use the back of this paper for notes)

___ Ask participants if they want a supporter.

___ Ask participants what they need from a Peacekeeper Conference.

___ Explain to participants what to expect when they are in the Peace Room.

___ Schedule time in the Peace Room:

Date: _____ Time: _____

Contact Jen Williams, author of *Peacekeepers, An Implementation Manual for Empowering Youth Using Restorative Practices,* at peacekeepers.jenwilliams@gmail.com for a download link containing this form.

Putting It All Together

Peacekeepers meet individually with all students involved in the conflict. They start with the offender to make sure he/she admits to their part in the conflict and is willing to participate in the Peacekeeper Conference. Then, they meet with the student who was harmed. Each student may bring a supporter to the Peace Room. This could be a friend or a staff member. The supporters do not get interviewed at the Pre-Meeting. I typically meet with the supporters separately to prepare them for what to expect in the Peace Room.

A word of Caution: Students often try to invite multiple friends to the Peace Room. Try to limit students to just the main players in the conflict. This helps focus the process and limits a ripple effect of extraneous issues surfacing. Students are encouraged to complete a new referral form if they feel the need to bring in other students.

Also, as mentioned previously, students at the middle level often have conflicts and they are developmentally focused only on themselves. It is important for the program coordinator to meet with the Peacekeeper team after the Pre-Meeting to discuss what questions will be asked during the conference.

Peacekeeper Conference Script

Peacekeepers each have their own unique copy of the script.

Helpful hints:

a. Peacekeepers write the participants' names where they are in the script to eliminate any on-the-spot thinking that could throw off the facilitator.

b. Laminate the script for each Peacekeeper.

c. Practice, practice, practice.

There is a possibility that students who seek help from the Peacekeepers have a mutual conflict. Many middle school conflicts do not have a clear offender and a person who was harmed. It is possible that both students involved feel as if they were harmed by the other. In this case, it is important for the students to have a voice as the offender and the person harmed. They answer questions one and two in the script.

Putting It All Together

Training Note: I invite past Peacekeepers to return to give peer feedback for those learning the script in a mock training conflict. Students take turns running through the script while classmates act through a conflict, taking on the roles found in the script. The classmates are encouraged to be a little difficult in order to challenge the facilitator a bit.

Two rubrics are completed by the past Peacekeepers to provide feedback for the class role-playing scenarios. I explain the importance to demonstrate competency with the script, that the administration of the school expects Peacekeepers to take this process seriously.

As the adult leader, you need to consider a few things each time the students work in the Peace Room. You may wish to say a few things after everyone is seated, before the conference begins. First, let the students know your role during the conference and that you will be in the room, but not in the circle unless the group needs support. Second, set expectations about confidentiality and that you are a mandated reporter and will handle any concerns about abuse privately with the student of concern. And last, show the students a talking piece and how to use it.

The rubrics are found on the following pages.

PEACEKEEPERS

Peacekeeper Facilitator/Notetaker Rubric

Name: _____

to evaluate Active Listening

1	2	3	4
Facilitator is disengaged	Facilitator gave their opinion and showed sympathy, not empathy.	Facilitator faced participants and made appropriate eye contact.	Facilitator showed appropriate empathy throughout
	Facilitator appeared distracted	Facilitator responded accurately	Facilitator remained objective

to evaluate Asking Questions

1	2	3	4
Facilitator doesn't follow questions as discussed after holding pre-meeting	Facilitator skipped and left out some questions	Facilitator asked all questions	Facilitator was able to manage difficult students
	Facilitator interjected their own opinion, using the words, "you should"	Facilitator stayed objective and unemotional, and used words like "you may consider…"	

to evaluate the Notetaker

1	2	3	4
Notetaker did not complete the agreement form and was unable to contribute to the group process.	Notetaker missed a solution while the group was discussing ideas for the plan.	Agreement is a one-step written agreement	Agreement is developed with a step by step, multiple scenario plan with input from all participants

Participant Behavior Rubric

Name: _____

Active Participation

1	2	3	4
Student is disengaged	Student is off task	Student cooperated with the facilitator	Student participated fully and supported the facilitator with valuable feedback

Participation in Multiple Roles

1	2	3	4
Student is disengaged	Student only plays one part in the script during the class	Student plays multiple roles during the class	Student plays multiple roles and provides feedback to the process

Appropriate Storytelling

1	2	3	4
Student is disengaged	Student mostly gives very short answers during the script	Student answers questions from the facilitator and adds some detail to their part	Student is eager to participate and gives great detail that helps strengthen their part in the conflict
Student is difficult to the process and doesn't know when to stop (more than 2 suggestions from facilitator to change behavior)	Student is difficult to the process and needs 2 reminders from the facilitator to stop	Student is difficult to the process and listened to the facilitator to stop	Student provides feedback to the facilitator after being a "difficult student" that is helpful for the facilitator to work through handling difficult students.

The Peacekeeper Conference Script

"Welcome. My name is _____ and I will be facilitating this meeting. Do you know why you are here today?

        YOUR NAME

    Pause for response.

"We received an incident report with your names on it. No one is in trouble, but we want to give you an opportunity to talk about your conflict. Is that ok with you?"

    Now introduce each conference participant and state his/her relationship to the offender or person harmed.

"Thank you for wanting to resolve your conflict with the Peacekeepers. This is a chance for you to resolve your conflict and repair the harm that has been done."

"This meeting will focus on a conflict that happened.

    Read a summary of the incident report and/or notes from the pre-meeting.

"It is important to understand that we will focus on what was done and how that behavior has harmed others. We are not here to decide whether you are good or bad. We want to explore in what way people have been affected and hopefully work toward repairing the harm that has resulted. Does everyone understand this?"

Putting It All Together

1. Say to offender:

"I must tell you that you do not have to participate in this conference and are free to leave at any time, as is anyone else. If you do leave, the matter may be referred to the office."

"The conflict may also be resolved through this process so we encourage you to fully participate. Do you all understand?"

2. Offender [Student one]

"We'll start with _____."
STUDENT ONE'S NAME

- *"What happened?"*

- *"What were you thinking about at the time?"*

- *"What have you thought about since the incident?"*

- *"Who do you think has been affected by your actions?"*

- *"How have they been affected?"*

PEACEKEEPERS

3. Ask the student who was harmed [Student two]

- "_____, what was your reaction at the time of the incident?"
  _{STUDENT TWO'S NAME}

- "How do you feel about what happened?"

- "What has been the hardest thing for you?"

- "How did your family and friends react when they heard about the incident?"

4. Ask the Supporter of student who was harmed
[If there are no supporters, still ask the last question]

- "What did you think when you heard about the incident?"

- "How do you feel about what happened?"

- "What has been the hardest thing for you?"

- "What do you think are the main issues?"

Putting It All Together

5. Ask the Supporter of the Offender

· *"What did you think when you heard about the incident?"*

· *"How do you feel about what happened?"*

· *"What has been the hardest thing for you?"*

· *"What do you think are the main issues?"*

6. Ask the Offender [student one]

"Is there anything you want to say at this time?"

7. Reaching an Agreement.

Ask the student who was harmed [student two]:

"What do you need from _____ to make things right with you?
STUDENT ONE'S NAME

Is there anything _____ can do to make it better for you?"
STUDENT ONE'S NAME

Ask student one the same questions.

"What do you need from _____ to make things right with you?
STUDENT TWO'S NAME

Is there anything _____ can do to make it better for you?"
STUDENT TWO'S NAME

At this point, all the participants discuss what should be in the final agreement. The Notetaker writes their plan on the Peacekeeper Conference Agreement.

It is important that you ask each student if they agree with each suggestion before the group moves to the next suggestion, asking

"What do you think about [repeat what was suggested]?"

If they do not agree, ask for more suggestions from the students or offer your own suggestion. Do not force an apology.

As you sense that the agreement discussion is drawing to a close, the Notetaker says to the participants:

"Before I prepare the written agreement, let me paraphrase what has been discussed so far."

Read the items in the agreement aloud and look to the participants for acknowledgment. Make any necessary corrections.

Putting It All Together

Closing the Conference

"Before I formally close this conference, I would like to provide everyone with a final opportunity to speak. Is there anything anyone wants to say? Is everyone ok with the agreement?"

Allow for participants to respond and when they are done, say:

"Thank you for what you said today. Congratulations on finding a solution to the conflict we discussed today. Please remember that what is said in here, stays in here and to keep things confidential.

"We also like to put name tags onto the peace sign as a way to show our larger community and all the people who work through conflicts like you did today. Please take a moment to place your name tag to the peace sign while we prepare an agreement that you will sign that explains what you decided is your plan moving forward."

Modified from the Conference Facilitator's Script for use with Student Facilitators: O'Connell, T., Wachtel, B. & Wachtel, T. (1999). Conferencing Handbook: The New Real Justice Training Manual. Pipersville, PA: Piper's Press.

Each year, the peace sign is covered more and more with names tags of those helped in the Peace Room.

Putting It All Together

PEACEKEEPERS

Peacekeeper Conference Agreement

Date _____

Name of individuals involved in the conflict: Grade:

_____   _____

_____   _____

_____   _____

_____   _____

Briefly describe the conflict:

_____

_____

_____

_____

_____

_____

_____

_____

Facilitators: _____

Agreement:

_____

_____

_____

_____

Signature of Victim/Supporter:

_____   _____

Signature of Offender/Supporter:

_____   _____

This agreement is confidential. Anything discussed outside of the Peace Room may result in an office referral.

Contact Jen Williams, author of *Peacekeepers, An Implementation Manual for Empowering Youth Using Restorative Practices,* at peacekeepers.jenwilliams@gmail.com for a download link containing this form.

Putting It All Together

The **Peacekeeper Conference Agreement** *(at left)* is a way for the participants to have a contract that describes the plan moving forward. The form is kept in a file box with the other documents of the case. The file box is housed in my locked office. Since the Peace Room is at a separate location then my office, I prefer to keep the documents with me at all times. Confidentiality is very important to maintain. I suggest not giving the students a copy of the entire form. I might make a copy of the agreement section if they want a copy. This limits the possibility of the situation to be out in the school community.

PEACEKEEPERS

Follow-Up Meeting Notes

Group: _____ Date: _____

Participant Name: _____

Case # _____

Read the "Briefly describe the conflict" section of the referral form to participant. Confirm the participants involved in conflict.

Review the Agreement that was made in the Peace Room (found on agreement form).

Ask the question: Are there any changes needed to support this agreement at this current time?

    __ No changes needed.

    __ The following changes are requested:

_____

_____

Ask the question: What support do you need from us today in order to move beyond this conflict? Check what applies to the student.

    __ There is a new conflict with this group that needs help.

    __ All is good; no check-ins needed.

    __ Things are good now, but I will request another Peacekeeper Conference if things get bad again.

Take notes here if needed:

_____

_____

Contact Jen Williams, author of *Peacekeepers, An Implementation Manual for Empowering Youth Using Restorative Practices,* at peacekeepers.jenwilliams@gmail.com for a download link containing this form.

Putting It All Together

The **Follow-Up Meeting Notes** *(at left)* is how the Peacekeepers check in with the students to see how the plan is working. It is rare that the conflict continues. Most of the cases end with the initial conference.

This check-in with participants gives students an extra layer of support. They appreciate knowing older kids are looking out for them and want to help them.

All of the forms are kept throughout the entire year and the data tracking sheet is provided to the office for state reporting.

PEACEKEEPERS

End-of-Year Peacekeeper Program Evaluation

Please provide feedback for the Peacekeeper Program.

List one thing that you remember most about the Peacekeeper Training.

Did you feel prepared as a Peacekeeper in 8th grade? Is there anything you needed to learn before starting in 8th grade that you didn't learn in the Peacekeeper Training?

In what ways have you grown as a Peacekeeper?

What would your friends say about how you have changed since becoming a Peacekeeper?

What is your favorite part of the program?

Share your favorite memory while being a Peacekeeper.

What advice would you give new Peacekeepers about the program?

What needs to change about the program?

Do you have any other ideas or thoughts that you would like to share with (Program Coordinator's Name) to improve the program?

Contact Jen Williams, author of *Peacekeepers, An Implementation Manual for Empowering Youth Using Restorative Practices,* at peacekeepers.jenwilliams@gmail.com for a download link containing this form.

Putting It All Together

Every year the students end with a celebration off site. I ask the group to come up with location options and we vote as a group. Some examples are stand up paddle boarding, swimming and kayaking, all with picnics to reflect on the year's work. I come prepared with small gifts for each Peacekeeper and data to show how many students they helped that school year.

It is an amazing moment, watching the students reflect on their growth and experiences in the program. They often fight over who gets to speak first. There are tears and laughs with sharing memories. It is my favorite part of the program.

The **End-of-Year Peacekeeper Program Evaluation** *(at left)* gives me feedback. I am always striving to improve the program. Don't be afraid to hear what the students have to say. It just might fill you up!!

PEACEKEEPERS

Bibliography

Dary, T., & Pickeral, T. (2013). School Climate Practices for Implementation and Sustainability. A School Climate Practice Brief, Number 1, and New York, NY: National School Climate Center.

 https://www.issuelab.org/resources/15024/15024.pdf

DuPaul, G., McGoey, K., & Yugar, J. (1997). Mainstreaming students with behavior disorders: The use of classroom peers as facilitators of generalization. School Psychology Review, 26(4), 634-650.

 https://www.tandfonline.com/doi/abs/10.1080/02796015.1997.12085891

Elias, M. (2004). The connection between social-emotional learning and learning disabilities: Implications for intervention. Learning Disability Quarterly, 27(1), p. 53-73.

 https://files.eric.ed.gov/fulltext/EJ704973.pdf

Goodwin, S., & Young, A. (2013). Ensuring children and young people have a voice in neighbourhood community development. Australian Social Work, 66(3), 344-357.

 https://www.tandfonline.com/doi/abs/10.1080/0312407X.2013.807857

Bibliography

Johnson, D. W., & Johnson, R. T. (2001). Teaching students to be peacemakers: A meta-analysis. Paper presented at the Annual Meeting of the American Educational Research Association, Seattle, WA.

http://eric.ed.gov/?q=teaching+students+to+be+peacemakers&id=ED460178

Kim, W. C. & Mauborgne, R (2003, January. Fair Process: Managing in the knowledge economy. Harvard Business Review, 81 (1), 127-136.

https://hbr.org/2003/01/fair-process-managing-in-the-knowledge-economy

O'Connell, T., Wachtel, B. & Wachtel, T. (1999). Conferencing Handbook: The New Real Justice Training Manual. Pipersville, PA: Piper's Press.

https://www.amazon.com/Conferencing-Handbook-Justice-Training-Manual/dp/0963388754

Schumacher, A. (2014). Talking circles for adolescent girls in an urban high school: A restorative practices programs for building friendships and developing emotional literacy skills. *SAGE Open*, 4, 1-13.

https://journals.sagepub.com/doi/full/10.1177/2158244014554204#:~:text=Findings%20demonstrated%20that%20Talking%20Circles,led%20to%20greater%20self%2Defficacy.

Wachtel, T., O'Connell, T., & Wachtel, B. (2010). Restorative justice conferencing: Real justice & the Conferencing handbook (pp.55, 228-230, 174-175). International Institute for Restorative Practices.

https://store.iirp.edu/restorative-justice-conferencing-real-justice-the-conferencing-handbook/

About the Author

Jen Williams (she/her) has 20 years experience working with middle level youth, primarily as a school counselor. Mrs. Williams earned her M.Ed from Villanova University and her M.S. from The International Institute for Restorative Practices, where she is an instructor and systemic coach for schools across the country. She holds a state board position with the Pennsylvania Association for Middle Level Education and serves on the Schools to Watch state team. Her passion is empowering young people to be part of the solution. Mrs. Williams resides in Chester County, Pennsylvania with her husband and two children.

peacekeepers.jenwilliams@gmail.com
linkedin.com/in/jennifer-williams-77047389/

PEACEKEEPERS

Made in the USA
Middletown, DE
29 September 2023